03|98-12x-12|97
6/05 27x 6/05

LOS GATOS PUBLIC LIBRARY

Reading About
THE RIVER OTTER

Carol Greene

Content Consultant:
Dan Wharton, Ph.D., Curator
New York Zoological Society

Reading Consultant:
Michael P. French, Ph.D.,
Bowling Green State University

ENSLOW PUBLISHERS, INC.
Eloy St. & Ramsey Ave.
Box 777
Hillside, N.J. 07205
U.S.A.

P.O. Box 38
Aldershot
Hants GU12 6BP
U.K.

Library of Congress Cataloging-in-Publication Data

Greene, Carol.
     Reading about the river otter / Carol Greene.
          p.   cm. — (Friends in danger series)
     Includes index.
     Summary: Describes the river otter and its behavior, explains its
status as an endangered species, and suggests what can be done to
help save it.
     ISBN 0-89490-425-6
     1. Lutra canadensis—Juvenile literature. 2. Endangered species
—Juvenile literature. [1. Otters. 2. Rare animals.] I. Title.
II. Series: Greene, Carol. Friends in danger series.
QL737.C25G77 1993
599.74′447—dc20   92-26801
                                                                 CIP
                                                                  AC

Printed in the United States of America

10 9 8 7 6 5 4 3 2 1

Photo Credits: ©The Bettmann Archive, p. 20; ©Denver Bryan, pp. 1, 4, 6, 8, 18, 24;
©Robert Lankinen/The Wildlife Collection, pp. 10, 16; ©Tom and Pat Leeson, pp. 12, 22;
©Thelma Shumsky/The Image Works, p. 26; ©Helen Williams/Photo Researchers, p. 14.

Cover Photo Credit: ©Tim Davis/Photo Researchers, Inc.

Photo Researcher: Grace How

CONTENTS

SLIP AND SLIDER

Winter is here
The night is cold.
Snow lies on the ground.
Out of their hole pops
a family of river otters.

The otters' den is
in the bank of a stream.
The hole is under water.

An adult otter peeks out from the icy water
of a stream.

A few months ago,
the young otters, or kits,
didn't want to swim.
Their mother, Slider,
had to help them.
Sometimes the kits rode
on the mother's back.

But now they like to swim,
even in very cold water.
Their thick fur
and fat under their skin
keep them warm.

A young kit peeks out of its den.

Their long bodies,
pointed tails, and webbed feet
make them wonderful
swimmers.

Slip and Slider lead
the kits down the stream.

"Chirp!" says Slip.
"Chirp!" says a kit.
River otters chirp
to keep track of one another
as they travel.

An otter chirps to find its mate.

Slip swims slowly
with his head above water.
Then he sees a fish.

Down he dives.
His feet and tail
help him twist and turn.
Soon he catches the fish.

An otter dives under the water.

River otters eat fish,
crayfish, clams, frogs,
snails, turtles, insects,
and other animals.

The kits drank Slider's milk
until they were four months old.
But now they can
catch their own food too.

An otter nibbles on a fish.

After the family has eaten.
Slip tosses a clam shell
into the air with his nose.
It falls into the water
and he dives for it.
Otters love to play.

Three river otters wrestle.

Slider climbs out
of the stream.
If there were no snow,
she would run slowly
on the land.

But now she runs
a few steps
then slides on her belly.
Run—slide. Run—slide.
River otters can go
18 miles an hour that way.

Slider finds a snowy slope.
Down she goes.
Splash! She hits the water.

An otter rests on a snow bank.

Soon Slip and the kits
are sliding too.
River otters often slide
down slopes just for fun.

When spring comes,
the kits will leave.
They will find mates
and start their own families.

But on this winter night,
they play together,
a happy, sliding family
of river otters.

A pair of otters.

DANGER!

Once, river otters lived
in most of North America.
But there were never
very many of them.

Then people began
to catch them in traps.
They wanted the otter's
thick, dark brown fur.

In the 1800s trappers caught otters all over
North America.

Now there are no
river otters in some parts
of the western and central
United States.

Several states have put
river otters on their list
of animals in danger.

People also take away
the wet places
where river otters live.
They drain the water
and plant crops or
build buildings.

Otters need wet places to live.

Sometimes people dump
trash and poisons into
rivers, streams, and lakes.
This kills the otters' food.
It can kill the otters too.

People must stop
killing otters for fur.
They must stop
taking away wet places.
And they must clean up
rivers, streams, and lakes.

With our help,
there will always be
happy, sliding otters.

A scientist brings otters to a new home.

WHAT YOU CAN DO

1. Learn more about
   river otters (sea otters too).
   Read books and watch nature
   shows.

2. Visit river otters
   at a zoo, if you can.
   They're fun to watch.

3. Don't buy or ask for anything
   made with the fur of any
   animal in danger.

4. Never throw trash
   into the water.
   Put all trash where it belongs.

Look for river otters next time you
visit a zoo.

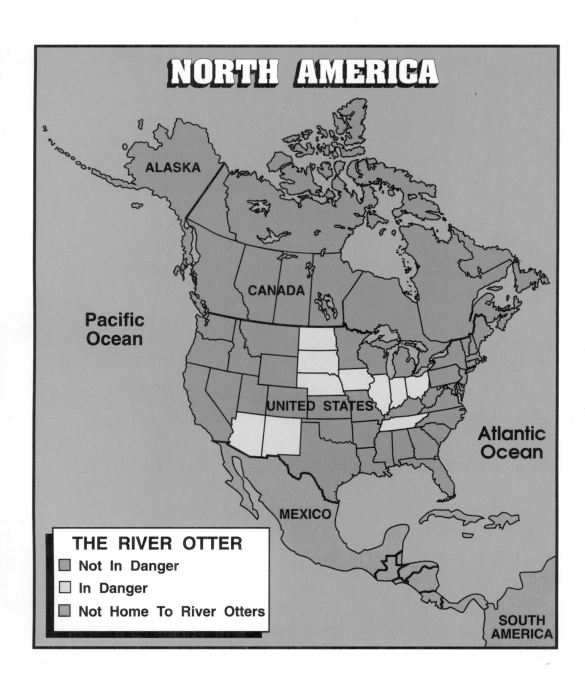

NORTH AMERICA

ALASKA

Pacific
Ocean

CANADA

UNITED STATES

Atlantic
Ocean

MEXICO

THE RIVER OTTER
Not In Danger
In Danger
Not Home To River Otters

SOUTH
AMERICA

MORE FACTS ABOUT THE RIVER OTTER

- River otters are 3 to 4-½ feet long. A foot or more of that is tail.

- They weigh from 10 to 25 pounds. Males are larger than females.

- River otters are dark brown on top and light brown or gray underneath.

- They often live in a den built by some other animal, such as a beaver or muskrat. They mostly come out at night.

- River otters can stay under water for 3 or 4 minutes without breathing.

- The female has from 2 to 4 kits sometime between January and May.

- River otters are related to weasels.

- They can live to be 19 years old.

WORDS TO LEARN

bank—The rising ground at the edge of a stream.

clam—A water animal that lives in a shell.

crayfish—A water animal that looks like a small lobster.

den—A resting place for animals. For river otters, it is a little room dug out under the ground.

drain—To take away water.

endangered—In danger of disappearing from the earth forever.

kit—A baby river otter.

river otter—A long animal with thick fur. It is part of the weasel family. Its Latin name is *Lutra canadensis*.

webbed—Having skin or some other tissue between the fingers or toes. River otters and ducks both have webbed feet.

INDEX